Corporate governance

of listed companies in

Kuwait

A comparative study with United

Kingdom, Saudi and Qatar codes

2016

Dr. Abdullah Al-shebli

Table of Contents

Corporate governance of listed companies

1. Introduction

In the last fifty years, many changes have occurred in the style of company ownership depending on the country. Nationalised industries have been privatised, and there has been a move away from family-owned firm to firms with diverse shareholders made up of individuals and institutions. This separation sometimes causes bad behaviour by managers of parties involved on secondary markets[1], such as advisors, analysts, hedge funds, auditors, collective investment schemes (CIS),[2] market intermediaries (brokers or investment banks), market

---

[1] Securities markets can be divided into two markets. The first is a primary market; the second is a secondary market. The former deals with the issuers' transactions (selling of securities by issuers), while the latter has trading transactions (buying and selling issued securities); Alan Palmiter, *Securities Regulation: Examples and Explanations* (6th edn, Aspen Publishers 2014) 1.

[2] Pooling assets of a number of investors by professional independence managers.

operators and issuers (companies). A number of companies have been ruined as a result of poor corporate governance.[3]

As early as the 1970s (Maxwell, Guinness) a few corporate scandals started to emerge which highlighted the risk to an investor's shareholding from the irresponsible, negligent and even fraudulent or near fraudulent actions of those responsible for governing a company leading to a fall in company value and even its complete collapse.[4] This trend continued into the 21st century culminating in the 2008 financial crisis.[5]

Is corporate governance part of securities law[6] or is it part of a country's regulatory framework? The term Securities law suggests that this is a law about securities and it is.

---

[3] Bob Tricker, *The Economist: Directors, An A-Z Guide* (Profile Books 2009) 2.

[4] Bob Ticker, *Corporate Governance: Principles, Polices and Practices* (3rd edn, Oxford University Press 2015) 11
[5] ibid 15

[6] In some countries, such as the UK, securities law is part of financial regulation while in other countries, such as Kuwait, securities are regulated by separate and special laws called 'Securities Laws'.

However it is not the only such law. There are corporate laws which also have a bearing on securities. Therefore when discussing securities it is preferable to use the term Regulatory Framework which encompasses different laws and secondary legislation[7] all of which have a bearing on securities and holders thereof.

Securities law differs from others laws on two counts. For example, securities law only covers securities activities while other law covers securities and other commercial activities. In addition, company and accounting law covers listed and unlisted companies but not foreign listed companies, while securities law covers all listed companies whether foreign or national, but not unlisted national companies.

The methods of enforcing, supervising and policing compliance with securities law is also different. There is a

---

[7]secondary legislation is legislation delegated by an act of parliament. Secondary legislation consists of so-called Rules. It is very useful because it is speedy and saves parliament time. It is passed by people who understand the subject and it has the power to impose fines without going to court.

specific body responsible for the enforcement and supervision of compliance with securities laws. This area of law covers a mixture of statutory provisions also known as 'Hard Law' and voluntary provision known as 'Soft Law' such as the "Comply or Explain" principle, whereas other laws consist solely of 'hard law'.

Corporate governance taken as a whole is definitely part of the regulatory framework. However corporate governance is not a monolithic structure. It has different facets to it and some facets may fall within the scope of securities law and others within the scope of Company Law, or other statutory instruments (listing and disclosure rules) and codes of practice. Corporate governance may be broken down into a number of key areas or facets namely internal controls, institutional investment, role the effectiveness of non – executive directors, recruitment and development of non-executive directors, audit committees and board diversity.

In the 1990s a company's responsibilities for these key areas were bundled into so called Codes which became part of a country's regulatory framework for securities, complementing the existing components of that framework mentioned previously. In Kuwait Corporate Governance provisions became mandatory while in the UK some became mandatory and others discretionary on the principle of Comply or Explain.[8]

Having good corporate governance is one way to prevent and reduce the occurrence of company scandals in the future and ensuring that the company protects the value on behalf of shareholders.

Good corporate governance can play a significant role in addressing both of these issues. However, the effect of good corporate governance is not limited only to these issues, because corporate governance is multi-faceted, and other aspects of corporate governance affect listed companies, such as risk management, bribery, fraud, and poor board practice. In recent years, a number of scandals and collapses have not only reduced shareholders' financial investment, but have also affected other stakeholders, such as employees who have lost their jobs and, in many cases, their pension funds as well. Better enforcement methods of

---

[8] Andy Ryde, Murray Cox, *The Corporate governance review* (editor Willem Calkoen, 5th edn, Law Business Research Ltd 2015) 411

corporate governance compliance have the potential to reduce lapses of corporate governance and to boost investor confidence, economic efficiency and growth.

In companies in which ownership and management are separate, as in the case of listed companies, there is a danger that a director, by virtue of his powers, could put the company at risk or abuse his or her position.[9] This is a worldwide problem, as illustrated by the examples below.[10]

---

[9] Erik Vermeulen, 'Beneficial Ownership and Control: A Comparative Study - Disclosure, Information and Enforcement' (2013) OECD Corporate Governance Working Papers 7, 8 <http://www.oecd-ilibrary.org/governance/oecd-corporate-governance-working-papers_22230939> accessed 9 September 2013.

[10]

Year	Country	Company
2001	US	Enron
2003	Italy	Parmalat known as Europe's Enron
2008	UK	Royal Bank of Scotland (RBS)
2009	India	Satyam
2012	Japan	Olympus Corporation

Numerous scandals and collapses have occurred in different countries as a result of the shortcomings in the way that companies are operated. Therefore, it is clear that no country is immune from such problems, including Kuwait. Where gaps exist between owners and managers (separation of ownership and control),[11] corporate governance principles can be used as one method of improving the performance of listed companies.[12]

Christine Mallin, *Corporate Governance* (4th edn, Oxford University Press 2013) 2-7.

[11] There are various theories about what corporate governance means, but the predominant theory is the 'agency theory', which considers the shareholders to be the principals and the directors to be their agents. Thus, there is a separation of ownership and control; (ibid 16-18).

[12] Qatar's Corporate Governance Code 2009 tries to explain this by saying that shareholders delegate powers to the board of directors, because in practical terms it is difficult for the shareholders to manage the company. The members of the board of directors delegate to executives the daily decision-making. As a result of these mandates, company executives have more power than members of the board of directors and shareholders, and they also have access to the important information in the easiest and quickest way. On the other hand, members of the board are in a better position to get important information and to control the company than shareholders. Thus, members of boards and executives may take advantage of this gap to achieve personal benefits at the expense of shareholders.

The need for effective corporate governance rules is greater than ever before. The majority of such rules already exist in Kuwait, Qatar and Saudi, but they are not wide-ranging enough. Securities law can play a significant role in improving corporate governance, because of effective enforcement. In other words, the securities law could enhance the enforcement of corporate governance principles.

It is unrealistic to try to fill these gaps with mandatory rules and regulations. A diversity of enforcement is required that is partly voluntary[13] and partly mandatory, which is the approach adopted in the UK. Seventy countries have adopted corporate governance codes in some form or another.[14]

---

[13] Such voluntary enforcement is generally referred to as 'comply or explain' and is underpinned by a regulatory framework that asks companies to send a report annually to the shareholders about the extent to which the principles have been adhered to and, if not, why not.

[14] Brian Cheffins, 'Corporate governance LLM Cambridge, An introduction part 2 (3CL)' (Cambridge University I Tunes).

Good corporate governance has the potential to affect a company's overall success. Some say that there is a relationship between the success of the company and corporate governance. That is to say, that the more a company applies governance rules, the greater are the company's chances of success.[15] Corporate governance rules are designed to protect nations, because the behaviour of companies influences our daily lives by promoting economic growth.[16] Consequently, some codes, such as the Kuwaiti Code 2013, require companies to exercise corporate social responsibility.

Although corporate governance principles differ from one country to another, good corporate governance is important. Consequently, this book will define corporate governance and review some of its better known failures. It will consider some of the corporate governance principles in existence in the UK, Saudi and Qatar, and the enforcement methods in the UK, in order to compare them with measures in place in Kuwait.

---

[15] Andrew Chambers, *Corporate Governance Handbook* (5th edn, Bloomsbury Professional 2012) 351.

[16] ibid 3.

2. What is Corporate Governance?

This book will look at the definition and the principles of corporate governance.

2.1 Definition

Although the term 'corporate governance' is used every day in the financial press, it is a complex term, because it relates to various matters, such as law, economics, management, accounting and other subjects, and each field has its own developments. Corporate governance issues also include culture, ownership and legal arrangements.[17] Therefore, defining corporate governance is not straightforward.[18] There is no clear definition of corporate governance; it is multi-faceted. However, under the regulation of corporate governance, laws, rules and

---

[17] Christine Mallin (n 11) 15.

[18] Andrew Keay, *The Enlightened Shareholder Value Principle and Corporate Governance* (Routledge 2013) 6.

standards define the relationship between a company's management on the one hand and shareholders and stakeholders, such as bondholders, workers, suppliers, creditors and consumers, on the other hand.

Since the first version of the UK Corporate Governance Code was produced the generally accepted definition in the UK has remained, the following which was set out in the UK Corporate Governance Code 2014:

> Corporate governance is the system by which companies are directed and controlled. Boards of directors are responsible for the governance of their companies. The shareholders' role in governance is to appoint the directors and the auditors and to satisfy themselves that an appropriate governance structure is in place. The responsibilities of the board include setting the company's strategic aims, providing the leadership to put them into effect, supervising the management of the business and reporting to shareholders on their stewardship. The board's actions are subject to laws, regulations and the shareholders in general meeting.[19]

---

[19] <https://www.frc.org.uk/Our-Work/Publications/Corporate-Governance/UK-Corporate-Governance-Code-2014.pdf> accessed 24 June 2015.

From this definition, corporate governance is about the relationship between the board and the shareholders in governing and controlling the company

The GCC countries deal with the definition of corporate governance in different ways. For example, the Qatari legislature defines corporate governance as a system through which one can manage and control commercial companies in accordance with the Qatari Corporate Governance Code 2009. The rules of the QCGC determine the distribution of rights and responsibilities among the various stakeholders[20] in the company, such as the board of directors and managers, shareholders and other stakeholders, and describe the rules and procedures for making decisions about the company's affairs. This is similar to the UK definition. However, the Saudi Code

---

[20] In the stakeholder theory, the emphasis is not just on shareholders. The directors are seen as representing other groups. Stakeholders are any group or individual with an interest in the company's activities or performance, including suppliers, customers, employees, banks, shareholders, local communities, providers of credit, and government. Some stakeholders are related to the company directly, while others are related indirectly; Christine Mallin (n 11) 69-70.

2006 has no definition of corporate governance. The Kuwaiti legislature has defined governance in vague terms, stating that corporate governance is based on a set of rules that represent the foundation on which good governance practices in companies are based. These rules include a set of principles and methodology with the requirements needed to achieve the goals of governance. It seems that they define the code whilst trying to define corporate governance.

Although there is no fixed definition of corporate governance, the idea is based on two points. One is about control of the day to day operation and the other about the future direction of the business of the company. Controlling corporate governance can be likened to controlling a car, which involves controlling the steering wheel, the brake and the accelerator to ensure that the car reaches its destination.[21] This means that corporate governance rules have the potential to define the authority, the approach to risk management, and how to protect a company and investors. Consequently, corporate governance is about the

---

[21] Donald Nordberg, *Corporate Governance Principles and Issues* (SAGE 2011) 7.

relationship between the boards and managers and between the boards and its investors by guiding company actions and monitoring their performance.[22]

2.2 Aim of corporate governance

The objectives that the corporate governance codes seek to achieve vary from one country to another. According to the UK Code 2012, its goal is to deliver a company's long-term success by facilitating effective, entrepreneurial and prudent management. Corporate governance is about good management; it is not about the day-to-day operation of the company. It is about the board. The code is a guide to good management.

In Saudi Arabia, according to Article 1 of the Corporate Governance Code 2006, amended in 2010, the aim of the rules set out in section (a) is to guarantee the protection of the rights of the shareholders and the stakeholders. However, the Qatar 2009 Corporate Governance Code

---

[22] ibid 5.

states that the goals of the corporate governance rules are to protect the company from one of the most important risks to which it may be exposed, namely the failure and shortcomings in its performance and the achievement of personal benefits.[23] In Kuwait, Resolution No 25 of 2013 places the issuing of corporate governance rules under the control of the Capital Markets Authority. It states the importance of establishing proper rules for corporate governance to achieve justice, competitiveness and transparency in the market. Rules of governance here are about principles, systems and procedures that better protect shareholders. In addition, they state that good governance is based on the promotion of three points. First, ethical behaviour to ensure commitment to ethics and good professional conduct; second, oversight and accountability and finally, administrative organisation to ensure the proper

---

[23] The Qatari legislature pointed out examples of the personal interests of the members of the board of directors and executives, such as the appointment of relatives and friends who are not eligible; receiving excessive wages, salaries, allowances, and other benefits; contracting business transactions with companies on unfair terms; and concealing, misleading or giving incorrect information to achieve a personal interest or to cover inadequate work, according to the Qatar Corporate Governance Code 2009.

distribution of powers and responsibilities and the separation of functions.

According to Chambers 'Good governance means substance not just form, practices not just policies and performance not just conformance'.[24] Thus, good governance requires performance and application, so that it is not just an expression.

2.3 Corporate governance principles

A number of possible corporate governance areas have developed over time. These include board composition (leadership), board effectiveness, the role of board committees, risk management, remuneration, relationships with shareholders, bribery and corruption, IT governance, mergers and acquisition, succession planning, sustainability and climate change, and proxy access.

---

[24] Andrew Chambers (n 16) 349.

It is difficult to find fixed rules of governance that are suitable for every situation, because governance rules for protecting the nation differ from governance rules for shareholders and creditors, etc.[25] Corporate governance needs to be developed over time. For example, in the UK, the Financial Reporting Council (FRC)[26] has stated that, even though the level of corporate governance standards is high, there still is room for improvement.[27] After the

---

[25] Donald Nordberg (n 22) 54.

[26] The Financial Reporting Council (FRC) is an independent regulatory in the UK. One of the FRC mission is to promote high quality corporate governance by setting the code and monitoring its impact. In 2003 the FRC took responsibility for the UK corporate governance code. The FRC's board comprise of 14 members some of them executive and some non-executive members. The board has three committees. The first one is the Code and Standards Committee which advises the board on matter relating to codes, setting standards and policy questions. The second one is Executive Committee which advises the board on matter relating to strategic issues and provides day-to-day oversight of the work of the FRC. The third one is Conduct Committee which advises the board on matter relating to conduct activates to promote high-quality corporate reporting. <https://www.frc.org.uk/Home.aspx> accessed 24 June 2015.

[27] Financial Reporting Council (FRC), 'Development in Corporate Governance 2011: The Impact and Implementation of the UK Corporate Governance and Stewardship Codes' (December 2011) 1.

financial crisis of 2007/2008, Britain cannot say that its corporate governance is better than any other countries, although before the crisis it was arguable that the level of governance standards in Britain was better than anywhere else.[28] However, in the last ten years, corporate governance legislation has appeared in a number of countries to increase investor protection and confidence, especially in stock markets.[29]

Corporate governance principles do not remain static, but evolve with the surrounding developments and must continue to develop. For example, the Organisation for Economic Co-operation and Development (OECD) issued Principles of Corporate Governance in 1999. The OECD governments agreed to revise new principles in 2004.[30] Ensuring the basis for an effective corporate governance framework, ensuring the equitable treatment of shareholders (including minority and foreign shareholders),

---

[28] Andrew Chambers (n 16) 350.

[29] Christine Mallin (n 11) 26.

[30] Fianna Joesover and Grant Kirkkpatrick, 'The Revised OECD Principles of Corporate Governance and Their Relevance to Non-OECD Countries' (2005) 3.

protecting the rights of shareholders, disclosure and transparency, the role of stakeholders in corporate governance and the effective monitoring of and by the board (responsibilities of the board) are among the most important areas covered by corporate governance principles.[31]

In the UK 2012 Code there are main principles, supporting principles and provisions. There are five main principles (A-E) pertaining to leadership, effectiveness, accountability, remuneration and relations with shareholders. Accordingly, the UK code is a guide to effective board practice. Each main principle has supporting principles, and each supporting principle has provisions. For example, provision A.2.1 states that the same person should not exercise the roles of chairman and chief executive. The letter A refers to the first main principle, which is the 'Leadership Principle'. The number 2 is about the second supporting principle, which is the 'Division of Responsibilities'. The number 1 refers to what action should be taken or not taken by the company to comply with the code. What compels listed company to

---

[31] ibid 7-9.

comply with the code in the UK and the sanctions for failure to comply will be discussed later.

3. The Effect on investors of failures of corporate governance

There are different types of failure, such as poor risk management, fraud, fictitious transactions, corruption, financial manipulation (such as Libor manipulation), rogue trading and personal interest. The causes of the above problems are always due to mismanagement. In the UK, many scandals have occurred; for example, those involving BAE Systems, BP, Barclays, GlaxoSmithKline, HSBC, HBOS, the Royal Bank of Scotland, Standard Chartered and the Natural Resources Corporation.[32] Barclays alone has been responsible for several corporate failures, including selling retail customers largely redundant Payment Protection Insurance (PPI), tax scams, shifting toxic assets off the balance sheet into a new company

---

[32] 'Britain's corporate failures invited a governance revolution' <http://www.ianfraser.org/britains-scandalous-corporate-failures-invite-a-governance-revolution/> accessed 25 October 2013.

called Protium, secret payments to Middle East investors, the betrayal of corporate customers, hiding the movement of funds from Iran to the United States, poor investment advice, failing to provide accurate data, falsifying the Libor rate, inflating executive bonuses, mixing customer and proprietary assets and mis-selling interest rate swaps to small and medium-sized businesses (SMEs).[33]

It is thought that the reason for the corporate scandals is the result of the hijacking of management theory from the main economic opinions in the 1980s, by focusing on increasing shareholder returns, such as large dividends, at the expense of retaining and reinvesting profits, including research and development, which caused false economic progress beginning in the 1980s.[34] The failures were caused by management problems, not economic problems. As a result, corporate governance principles can be described as an

---

[33] 'The 12 Barclays scandals that cast doubt on Diamond's testimony' < http://www.ianfraser.org/move-on-you-crazy-diamond/> accessed 28 October 2013.

[34] Simon Caulkin, 'Management theory was hijacked in the 1980s' *The Guardian* (London, 28 June 2013) <http://www.guardian.co.uk/commentisfree/2012/nov/12/management-theory-hijacked > accessed 17 October 2013.

intervention in the management of the company that aims to reduce the likelihood of such company failures.

One of the main influences that affect a company's future is high risk management, of which there are several examples. The BP oil spill is a good example of poor risk management. Known as the 'Deepwater Horizon disaster', the incident in April 2010 occurred because BP ignored standard safety procedures to decrease the cost of delay that would have been approximately $1 million a day. The oil spill harmed shareholders, because the share price dropped dramatically, the company's profits declined and affected BP's employees, the environment, and the local community. Eleven people died and BP had to pay more than $14 billion for the cost of the clean-up.[35] The Gulf of Mexico environment was in crisis for 87 days as a result of the spill.[36]

---

[35] For more detail, see the new website that BP recently set up to defend its response. <http://www.thestateofthegulf.com/our-view/> accessed 10 November 2013.

[36] ibid.

Lynn Stout states that the drive to maximise shareholder value by focusing on short-term earnings affects stakeholder goals, including long-term investors. It stops the growth of the company as there is a conflict between the rising shareholder value and the development of the company. She mentions that the solution is to build good boards instead of shareholder value thinking.[37] The idea of focusing only on shareholder value did not exist fifty years ago, because the company goals were not the same. The focus was not only on shareholders, but also on providing greater protection to employees and society in general.[38] There is no law which requires managers to increase the share price of a company. The drive to do this is purely the doing of managers themselves.[39]

Without doubt, proper risk management is likely to decrease the occurrence of company scandals and

---

[37] Lynn Stout, *The Shareholder Value Myth: How Putting Shareholders First Harms Investors, Corporations, and the Public* (Berrett Koehler Publishers 2012) 83-85.

[38] ibid 3.

[39] ibid 4.

collapse.[40] There are four major risk groups, and each company must identify the four categories and the links between them, knowing what is acceptable and what the company can bear. The first group is comprised of financial risks, including debt and interest rates, poor financial management, asset losses, and accounting problems. This type can be controlled by the company. The second is comprised of operational risks, including poor capacity management, employee issues (fraud, bribery and corruption), and cost overruns. This group can also be controlled by the company. The third group is comprised of strategic risks, including such external factors as pricing pressure, partner losses and industry downturns. The fourth group is comprised of hazard risks, including political issues, natural disasters, terrorism and legal issues. The last two groups cannot be controlled by the company. This analysis shows that there are financial and non-financial risks.[41] The question here is how to protect investors from risk management by using corporate governance. Managers

---

[40] Luca Enriques and Dirk Zetzsche, 'The Risky Business of Regulating Risky Management In Listed Companies' (2013) European Company and Financial Law Review 10 (3) 1, 2.

[41] Alpesh Shah, 'Corporate Governance for Main Market and AIM companies' (2012) White Paper, London Stock Exchange 104.

can misuse their position to achieve something at the expense of the company that is not in the company's interests, such as gaining personal benefits, misbehaviour by managers, or just increasing the company's profits.

Some say that the core of the problem is caused by separating ownership and control in managing other people's money,[42] which is an agency theory. These problems may be avoided in the future by applying corporate governance principles. The question is how to find a proper way to enforce these principles. However, there is a danger that by introducing more regulations, economic growth will be affected. It is impossible to prevent such occurrences simply by passing laws and regulations. The quality of management must be improved to make it more ethical in an effort to stop managers engaging in and turning a blind eye to dishonest practices, with greater vigilance to stop others in the company from engaging in such practices.

---

[42] Alessio Pacces, *Rethinking Corporate Governance: The Law and Economics of Control Powers* (Routledge 2012) 3.

4. No One Size Fits All

It is true that one size does not fit all listed companies in the corporate governance regime. For example, in the UK standard listed and AIM-quoted companies have more flexibility about choosing what provisions they adopt than premium listed companies.[43] Moreover among premium listed companies there are differences in compliance requirements between big, small and mid-sized companies. This method of compliance will lead to development of the national stock exchange. The UK principles-based approach to corporate governance ensures the regime is valued and supports companies of all sizes because managers would do what is right for the company with ample room for firm choice that suits their own strategic and operational challenges.

---

[43]<http://www.londonstockexchange.com/companies-and-advisors/aim/publications/documents/corpgov.pdf> accessed 7 October 2015

The FRC and QCA Quoted Companies Alliance[44] agree about the regulatory burden for small listed companies and the QCA has advised the FRC to find a way of reducing the burden areas.[45] There are around 2000 small and medium size listed companies in the UK which represents about 85% of the listed companies in the UK.[46] From the number it can be said firstly that they are important to the liquidity and to the profits.

Secondly small companies with limited recourse would avoid the statutory requirements or try to withdraw from being listed on stock exchanges which would affect the growth of the economy as well as the stock exchange and the small companies.

---

[44] QCA is independent member body that champions the interest of small and medium size listed company on London Stock exchange. One of its aims is to reduce the regulatory burden. <http://www.theqca.com/about-us/> accessed 12 November 2015

[45] <http://www.theqca.com/article_assets/articledir_210/105491/QCARe sponseFRC_Improving_Quality_Reporting_Smaller_Listed_AIM_Qu oted_Companies_Jul15.pdf> accessed 12 Nov. 15

[46] <http://www.theqca.com/about-us/> accessed 12 Nov. 15

Small companies are the engines of economic growth. Small listed companies are important to the future development in the growth of the economy[47] Complying with compulsory rules is onerous for small and middle sized listed companies.[48] It is also a big challenge for small businesses because of the costs.[49] If small companies are not encouraged to list their shares they cannot receive funding from the stock exchange which is a flexible source of capital and this process would avoid bad debts.[50]

5. Corporate Governance in the UK

In the UK, corporate governance is regulated by a mixture of laws, rules and codes, such as the Company Act 2006, the Bribery Act 2010, the Financial Services and Market Act 2000 (FSMA), Listing Rules that apply the Corporate

---

[47]<http://www.theqca.com/article_assets/articledir_210/105491/QCAR esponseFRC_Improving_Quality_Reporting_Smaller_Listed_AIM_Qu oted_Companies_Jul15.pdf > accessed 12 Nov. 15

[48]ibid

[49] ibid.

[50]<http://www.ft.com/cms/s/0/1a905c28-0aad-11e5-98d3-00144feabdc0.html#axzz3rH8e9NO7> accessed 12 November 2015

Governance Code, business principles, the Takeover Code, and the Stewardship Code 2010. Some of these laws, rules and codes will be mentioned in later sections because of their effect on corporate governance in the UK. However, this section will discuss the UK Corporate Governance Code.

Among the most important codes relating to corporate governance in the UK are the UK Corporate Governance Code 2010 and the UK Stewardship Code 2010, the latter of which is related to institutional investors.[51] These investors can play a role in enforcing the corporate governance code and this will be shown later. Both are published by the Financial Reporting Council (FRC).[52] In September 2012, the FRC published the new edition of the UK Corporate Governance Code. The first corporate governance code was published in 1992 (the Cadbury Code) and changes have been made to the Code since that

---

[51] Institutional investors can play a significant role in corporate governance developments and enforcement, as can be seen clearly in the UK and the US, but they do not act as owners; Christine Mallin (n 11) 367.

[52] ibid 27.

time. The idea of 'comply or explain' by which a company has to comply with the code or explain why it has not, still exists, because it has flexibility (no one size fits all), and it works alongside the company law and listing rules to make the UK's among the highest corporate governance standards in the world.[53] After the Cadbury Code, there were a number of instruments, such as the Combined Code (1998) based on the 'comply or explain' idea (the company should comply with the law or explain the reason for its non-compliance). At that stage the code was purely voluntary,[54] however, now it is not. This will be discussed later. This was revised in 2003, updated in 2008 and reviewed in 2009. In 2010, the Combined Code was renamed the UK Corporate Governance Code and was issued with more changes.[55] However, there is no code that can stop company failures; codes can only reduce them.

---

[53] Chris Hodge, 'Corporate Governance for Main Market and AIM Companies' (2012) White Paper London Stock Exchange 8-9.

[54]< http://www.grant-thornton.co.uk/Global/Publication_pdf/Corporate_Governance_Review_2012.pdf > p6 accessed 25 June 2015

[55] ibid 29-35.

In 2013, the FSA's functions were taken over by the Financial Conduct Authority (FCA) and the Prudential Regulation Authority (PRA), as the result of which the FSA was renamed the FCA according to the Financial Services Act 2012, which amended the FSMA 2000. The FCA is responsible for 'conduct of business regulation' for all firms, while the PRA is responsible for prudential authority firms (such as banks, insurance, Lloyds of London, building societies, and some investment firms) for 'supervision' of prudential issues. 'Conduct of business regulation' means protecting investors, policing the market and promoting competition and protection for consumers.[56] The FCA is fully funded by the companies that it regulates,[57] and it works independently of the government. The Treasury appoints the board that manages the FCA. The Finance Reporting Council (FRC) is responsible for publishing the Corporate Governance Code. The FRC is a non-profit organisation in the form of a company limited by guarantee. Funded partly by government and partly by industry, the FRC's board is appointed by the Secretary of State for Business. The FRC is responsible for promoting

---

[56]   <http://uk.practicallaw.com/7-503-5430?service=fs#a857525> accessed 1 October 2013.

[57] <http://www.fca.org.uk/about>   accessed 25 June 2015

high quality corporate governance, and it is an independent regulator.[58] Many of the FRC's functions, including setting the UK Corporate Governance Code, are recognised in statute under the Company Act 2006 and the Companies (Audit, Investigations and Community Enterprise) Act 2004.[59] In April 2013, both the FCA and the FRC signed a Memorandum of Understanding (MoU) for co-operation and co-ordination. This MoU sets out their different responsibilities: '3-The FRC is responsible for promoting high quality corporate governance and reporting to foster investment, while the FCA is responsible for the integrity of the provision of financial services to users'.[60]

Listing rules can play a significant role in applying corporate governance rules. In 2011, the FSA passed new Listing Rule 9.8.6 R, which helped to apply the Corporate

---

[58] <http://www.frc.org.uk/> accessed 1 October 2013.

[59]<http://frc.org.uk/Our-Work/Publications/FRC-Board/Memorandum-of-Understanding-between-the-Financial.aspx> accessed 2 October 2013

[60] ibid.

Governance Code. This rule[61] required that the listed company include the way that it has applied the main principles in its annual financial report. It must also show that all relevant provisions have been complied with and, if not, a statement of why the company cannot comply.[62] In

---

[61] In the case of a listed company incorporated in the United Kingdom, the following additional items must be included in its annual financial report.

> (5) a statement of how the listed company has applied the 'Main Principles' set out in the UK Corporate Governance Code in a manner that would enable shareholders to evaluate how the principles have been applied;
>
> (6) a statement as to whether the listed company has: (a) complied throughout the accounting period with all relevant provisions set out in the UK Corporate Governance Code or (b) not complied throughout the accounting period with all relevant provisions set out in the UK Corporate Governance Code and, if so, setting out: (i) those provisions, if any, that it has not complied with; (ii) in the case of provisions whose requirements are of a continuing nature, the period within which, if any, it did not comply with some or all of those provisions; and (iii) the company's reasons for non-compliance...

[62] Andrew Chambers (n 16) 355.

the UK, application of these principles by using listing rules, which were discussed in chapter four, has produced successful results, and companies are beginning to realise the importance of the application of these principles according to the FRC Report 2011.[63]

As mentioned above, in the UK, there is a body (FRC) that develops corporate governance rules. Kuwait, Saudi Arabia and Qatar would benefit from having an organisation like the FRC to develop their codes.

6. 'Comply or Explain' Regime

A 'comply or explain' regime can be described as an alternative way to achieve strong regulation. It strikes a balance between soft law and hard law that can be suitable in today's complex economic world. The 'comply or explain' approach has both advantages and disadvantages. Michelle Edkins, who works in the field of corporate governance as Managing Director of Corporate Governance

---

[63] Financial Reporting Council (FRC) Development (n 28) 3.

and Responsible Investment at BlackRock Inc., summarises the advantages and disadvantages of this system by saying that:

> …"comply or explain" has its limitations, poor explanations, differences of opinion between management and shareholders, different views as to the right approach amongst shareholders, lack of resources for engagement, and limits on the scope of some shareholders to be pragmatic. Nonetheless, "comply or explain" offers more flexibility than the alternative. Companies have the opportunity to set out their case and, whether agreement is reached or not, engagement helps build mutual understanding. Communication about the future involves indicating plans to adopt and improve, which, for shareholders - the institutions and the private savers among our clients - provides reassurance that

companies are being run for the long-term and in the interests of the shareholders.[64]

In addition to investors, companies would benefit from a corporate governance code. According to the chairman of the London Stock Exchange, Chris Gibson-Smith, 'Companies benefit from visible, strong corporate governance practices by attracting more investors and so reducing the cost of capital for all'.[65]

'Comply or explain' means more flexibility in the application of the set of rules with no free passes for avoiding these rules. Companies are required to provide an explanation, and others, such as future investors and institutional investors, will judge and monitor. Although

---

[64] Michelle Edkins, 'Comply or Explain, An Essay on the Report Titled: Comply Or Explain: 20th Anniversary of the UK Corporate Governance Code' (London Stock Exchange, The Financial Reporting Council Limited 2012) 18.

[65] Chris Gibson-Smith, 'An Essay on the Report Titled 'Comply Or Explain': 20th Anniversary of the UK Corporate Governance Code' (London Stock Exchange, The Financial Reporting Council Limited 2012) 6.

there is no action from a regulatory authority if the explanation is insufficient, the market forces the shareholders to take action. The share price will force the shareholder to engage. Investing is about taking risks. An investor who buys stock in a company with high standards of corporate governance is less likely to lose money. This is discussed more fully in Chapter Five. Investment advisers will also take the statement of a code into account when giving advice.

The market in general and the shareholders specifically, force the companies to follow the code.[66] Simply, the process for shareholders is that if no one wants to buy the company's shares, then the price will decrease, which prompts the shareholders to try to correct the situation. Consequently, the decline in the share price encourages the firm to adopt good corporate principles. The process is similar to the idea of market power on competitive policy

---

[66] Andrew Keay, 'Comply Or Explain: In Need Of Greater Regulatory Oversight', (2012) SSRN Working paper <http://papers.ssrn.com/sol3/papers.cfm?abstract_id=2144132 > accessed 22 February 2014.

that drives firms to improve their prices and services.[67] Shareholders will consider this noncompliance when deciding to buy, vote, hold and sell their shares.[68]

The Code is under development. The Chairman of the Financial Reporting Council, Baroness Sarah Hogg, acknowledged that although the UK Code benefits the market, such as making a difference in the corporate culture, there is still work that needs to be done to develop the Code further.[69] Andrew Keay criticised the 'comply or explain' regime, because no regulatory body assesses the companies' statements and there is no way to measure the extent to which these principles actually work, such as statistics. Shareholders do not really engage in monitoring

[67] Massimo Motta, *Competition Policy: Theory and Practice* (Cambridge University Press 2009) 41.

[68] David Seidl, Paul Sanderson, John Robert 'Applying "Comply Or Explain": Conformance with Codes of Corporate Governance in UK and Germany' (2009) University of Cambridge working paper.

[69] Essay 'Comply Or Explain: 20th Anniversary of the UK Corporate Governance Code' (2012) London Stock Exchange, The Financial Reporting Council Limited 4-5.

their companies.[70] He suggested introducing regulatory oversight to examine whether each company complies and whether the explanations are adequate.[71]

One response to Keay's comment is that the content of the explanation is not important. For example, in Germany, the corporate governance code works under the 'comply or disclose' approach, under which the firms comply with the recommendations or disclose their noncompliance.[72] In the 'comply or disclose' approach, firms comply or just say they will not comply. Secondly, some provisions of the code are already in rules or law and are mandatory. The 'comply or explain' regime is part of a large regulatory system. The code can be used as clear evidence of not complying with other rules and laws. The third point is that there is already a mechanism for judging the adequacy of an explanation under the Stewardship Code, under which institutional investors must take action if they deem that an explanation is inadequate and they have to comply or explain any failure to take action. The Stewardship Code

---

[70] Andrew Keay (n 67).

[71] ibid.

[72] David Seidl, Paul Sanderson, John Robert (n 69).

aims to help institutional investors (on behalf of clients and beneficiaries) to exercise their responsibilities properly under the 'comply or explain' regime. Therefore, institutional investors will monitor their investee companies under a 'comply or explain' regime by, for example, giving a timely written explanation if, after careful consideration, they do not accept the company's position.[73] There is no stewardship code in the GCC countries. It would be better if there were a code under a 'comply or explain' system in these countries, which would rely on family companies to take action. The fourth point concerns enforcement of compliance by a regulatory authority. More rules will affect market competition.

---

[73] According to Principle 3 of the UK Stewardship Code 2012; 'Institutional Investors Should Monitor Their Investee Companies' <http://www.frc.org.uk/Our-Work/Publications/Corporate-Governance/UK-Stewardship-Code-September-2012.pdf> accessed 19 January 2014.

7. Corporate Governance in Kuwait, Qatar and Saudi

Corporate governance in Kuwait, Qatar and Saudi is lacking in two areas. First, coverage of the various areas of corporate governance, such as risk management, is inadequate. Secondly, the methods of enforcement of the corporate governance provisions that do exist can be improved.

7.1 Existing Corporate Governance Provisions relating to Listed Companies

In Kuwait, Qatar and Saudi, various laws affect companies. As in the UK, some laws apply to all companies, as do the Company Act 2006 in the UK, the Companies Act 1965 in Saudi Arabia, the Companies Act 2002 in Qatar, and the Companies Act 2013 in Kuwait. Other laws apply only to listed companies and are enforced by the capital market authorities in the respective countries, such as the FCA in the UK.[74]

All the above laws address issues of corporate governance either directly or indirectly. For example, the liabilities of directors and the rights of shareholders are usually contained in corporate law, while other aspects of corporate governance form part of statutory instruments, such as rules and codes, and legislation affecting listed companies. Sometimes there is an overlap between the two types of legislation namely corporate and securities legislation. When a company is listed in the same country as it is incorporated, the company will be subject to both sets of

---

[74] For example, according to Article 1 of the Kuwait Companies Act 2013, this act shall apply to companies incorporated in Kuwait or headquartered in Kuwait. Consequently, non-Kuwaiti listed companies are subject only to laws, rules and codes of the Kuwaiti Stock Exchange. If a UK company is listed on the Kuwaiti Stock Exchange, it must comply with the rules of the Kuwait Stock Exchange. The company's activities are in the UK even though it is listed on the Kuwaiti Stock Exchange. As a result, its activities must follow Kuwaiti company laws, although its listing must comply with the laws, rules and code of the London Stock Exchange. Consequently, the Kuwaiti company does not have to comply with the UK Company Act 2006.

legislation. However, if a company is listed on a stock exchange in a jurisdiction other than where it is incorporated, the jurisdiction in which the stock exchange is located can hold it accountable only according to statutory instruments that apply to that stock exchange.[75] This chapter will narrow its scope to the governance issues handled by capital market authorities, especially the codes.

---

[75] In Saudi Arabia, there are different laws, rules and codes, such as Shari'ah Law, the Companies Law 1965, the Capital Market Law 2003, listing rules, and the corporate governance regulations (the Code) 2006 that deal with corporate governance areas; Gonzalo Puig and Bader Al-haddab, 'The Protection of the Minority Shareholders in the Gulf Cooperation Council' (2013) 13(1) JCLS (123-149) 3.

Qatar has the Commercial Companies Law 2002, Law No. (8), the Qatar Financial Markets Authority 2012 listing and the Qatari Corporate Governance Code 2009 that deal with corporate governance areas.

Kuwait has the Companies Law 2013, the Securities Law 2010 and listing rules, disclosure rules and the Corporate Governance Regulations 2013 (the Code) that deal with corporate governance areas.

7.2 Kuwait, Qatar and Saudi Codes

In the UK, securities regulation contains the Corporate Governance Code published by the FRC and enforced by the FCA, formerly by the FSA. The UK adopted a principles-based approach to corporate governance rather than a rules-based approach. Sometimes there is an overlap with other rules, such as disclosure rules, or the principles needed to add separate rules, such as risk management, which will be discussed later. This means that companies whose shares are listed on the main markets of the London Stock Exchange Limited do not have to comply with the Code. However, if they decide not to comply, they must explain to their shareholders the reasons for non-compliance. Furthermore, they must include in their annual report and accounts two statements: (1) an explanation about how the company has applied the main and supporting principles; and (2) a statement about whether the company has complied with the provisions throughout the year covered by the report. If the company has not complied with all provisions or has complied with them for only part of the year, the company must state its reasons for non-compliance. See Appendix 2 for an example of such a statement.

The 'comply or explain' approach is a key feature of the UK 2012 Code. However, the GCC countries have different approaches to corporate governance and its enforcement. In Kuwait, compliance is mandatory, and failure to comply is a breach of Securities Law No 7 of 2010. Moreover, a company must send a quarterly report to the Kuwaiti Capital Market Authority confirming that it has complied with all of the corporate governance provisions. Qatar has adopted a 'comply or explain' approach, but the explanation must be provided to the Qatari Financial Market Authority (QFMA), not the shareholders, in the form of an annual report. Nevertheless, the filing enables the company's shareholders and the public to assess the company's commitment to the principles of corporate governance.[76] In 2006, the Saudi Corporate Governance Code was introduced based on the 'comply or explain' approach. However, over time, certain of the original provisions have become mandatory. For instance, in 2008, 2010, 2011 and 2012, Articles 8, 15, 10 and 5 respectively

---

[76] Qatari Code 2009, Article 2.

were changed to compulsory rules. It would have been better if mandatory and voluntary provisions had not been mixed in the same code. Explanation for non-compliance with the voluntary provisions must be made to the shareholders, although the company must include a corporate governance statement in its annual board report.[77]

Although the codes of Kuwait, Qatar and Saudi have principles, supporting principles and provisions, they are not the same in each country.

7.2.1 Corporate Governance Principles in Kuwait, Qatar and Saudi

No common corporate governance principles are enforced in all of the states. These principles differ from country to country. For example, the principles of corporate governance mentioned in the Qatar Rules 2009 are intended to protect the interests of minority shareholders and to govern the responsibilities of the board of directors,

---

[77] Saudi Code 2009, Article 1 part C, Article 9 part A.

accounting and auditing, transparency of ownership and control, and the regulatory environment. However, in Kuwait, the Corporate Governance Code is extensive. Resolution No 25 of 2013 includes eleven principles that strengthen board composition, establish clear roles and responsibilities, recruit highly qualified candidates for boards of directors and senior management, safeguard integrity in financial reporting, require sound systems of risk management and internal controls, promote ethical standards and responsible conduct, ensure timely and high quality disclosure, recognise the legitimate interests of stakeholders, encourage enhanced performance, stress the importance of social responsibility[78] and finally protect the rights of shareholders.[79]

---

[78] That could happen, for example, when the company is working to achieve a balance between the objectives of the company and the community in the context of assistance in providing job opportunities, supporting small projects, protecting the environment from pollution, contributing to the reduction of the negative phenomena in society, etc. according to Kuwaiti Corporate Governance Code 2013.

[79] An example of such protection is not to have shareholder funds expropriated by the managers of a company.

However, the Saudi 2006 Corporate Governance Code has fewer principles than Kuwait and Qatar. It focuses on three areas according to Governance Code 2006. Part 2 of the Code mentions rights of shareholders and the general assembly, part 3 requires disclosure and transparency, and, finally, part 4 provides board of director principles.

Under each of the main principles are supporting principles. For instance, in the UK, under the first main 'leadership principle', there are four supporting principles, namely the role of the board, division of responsibilities, the chairman and finally non-executive directors.

7.2.2 Corporate Governance Sub-Principles in Kuwait, Qatar and Saudi

There are differences in the sub-principles among the GCC countries, such as those relating to board committees. One of the most important supporting principles under corporate governance codes is to form committees.[80]

---

[80] Examples of committees:

Kuwait requires the formation of five committees, while Qatar requires only three and Saudi Arabia requires two. According to Kuwaiti Corporate Governance Code 2013, each board must form five different types of committee:

> (1) Audit Committee: According to principle 4/2, the board of directors must form a committee

---

A. Audit Committee

In modern business, internal audit plays a significant role in corporate governance, because the management does not have sufficient knowledge and time it delegates some tasks to an internal auditor. This is simply an internal job, which is part of the management's tasks. The audit committee, acting on behalf of the board, monitors the quality of both external and internal audits; Andrew Chambers (n 16) 380-38.

One problem that could be solved by the audit committee is to require the committee to report the way they are selected by the external auditor; Financial Reporting Council (n 28) 19.

B. Remuneration Committee

More transparency is required in the remuneration committee report in terms of the remuneration plan, company policy, the risk and the link among these things; ibid 19.

c. Nominations committee

Nomination is an important point, because a person could be loyal to the person who appointed him, so that he could give that person information from the board.

concerned with internal audit. Its primary role is to ensure the integrity of the financial reporting and internal control systems and to recommend the nomination of the external auditor to the board. Thereafter, the general assembly appoints the external auditor in accordance with the nomination of the board of directors.

(2) Risk Management Committee: The company must form a committee concerned with risk management according to principle 5/2.

(3) Governance Committee: The board of directors must form a committee concerned with the application of governance according to principle 5/4.

(4) Nomination Committee: According to principle 3/1, the board of directors must form a committee concerned with nominations for appointment. Its primary role is to prepare recommendations on all proposed nominations to achieve the perfect selection of competent people with professional expertise and technical capacity for the board of directors and senior management.

(5) Remuneration Committee: According to principle 3/2, the board of directors must form a committee concerned with bonuses, its primary role being the development of policies and regulations for granting compensation and bonuses.

It should be noted that, in Kuwait, the formation of committees is the responsibility of the board of directors and is not limited to the above committees. The board of directors can form any other committees that it deems necessary for the company in accordance with principle 2/2 of the Kuwaiti Corporate Governance Code 2013, which states that the board of directors must form specialised and independent committees to help the board achieve its tasks.

According to Article 5 of the Qatar Corporate Code 2009, the board is allowed to delegate some of its powers and to form special committees to do specific operations, although the board remains responsible for all of the powers and authority that it delegates. The board shall form three committees, which are the Nominations Committee, the Remuneration Committee and the Audit Committee, as provided in Articles 15, 16 and 17 respectively.

In Saudi Arabia, the board determines the suitable number of committees that are needed, although two committees are required. In 2008, an audit committee was required, and, in 2010, a nomination and remuneration committee was required. Kuwait and Qatar separate the nomination and remuneration committees, while Saudi Arabia puts both in one committee.

7.2.3 Corporate Governance Provisions in Kuwait, Qatar and Saudi

The corporate governance codes in Kuwait, Qatar and Saudi not only differ at the principle and sub-principle levels, but they also differ in terms of the provisions that make up the principles and sub-principles. The differing provisions relating to board composition will be highlighted below.

One of the corporate governance principles is to strengthen board composition, which contains a number of points, including diversity (directors with different experience and attributes and even gender), independence (including independent and non-executive directors), and board election.[81] To achieve this goal, a number of provisions must be followed, including, for example, ensuring that directors are independent.[82]

In Kuwait, provision 1.1.C of the 2013 Code provides that the majority of the members of the board of directors must be non-executive members and that the board must include independent members, although the number of independent directors cannot exceed half the number of board members. In Qatar, Article 9, provision 2, states that a third of the directors must be independent directors. In Saudi Arabia,

---

[81] In Kuwait, one of the principles that is taken into account when forming the board of directors is diversity in experience, professional and competent skills, and members also have to know the laws, regulations, and the rights and duties of the board of directors, according to Rule One of the Kuwaiti Corporate Governance Code 2013.

[82] An independent member is a member who is not under the influence of anything that limits his ability to make decisions objectively and impartially, based on the facts only. For example, an independent member does not work in the company and is not a relative of one of the members of the senior management executive, according to article 1 of the Qatari Corporate Governance System 2009.

Article 12, provision (e), states that the board includes two independent directors or one-third of the board, whichever is greater.

In the UK, provision B.1.2 distinguishes between the FTSE 350 companies, which are large companies, and small companies. The board of the latter is required to contain at least two independent non-executive directors, while at least half of the former board must be comprised of independent directors.

Another example of differences among Kuwait, Qatar and Saudi concerns the re-election of directors. Kuwait provision 1.1.b and Saudi Article 12, provision 2, provide for the same re-election period not to exceed three election years and that a director may be re-elected unless the Articles of Association provide otherwise. In the UK, an annual re-election is required according to provision B.7.1 of the 2012 code.

The third example concerns the number of directors. In Saudi Arabia, Article 12, entitled 'Formation of the Board', has nine provisions. For example, a provision mentions that the number of directors shall not be fewer than three and not more than eleven, as specified in the Articles of Association. In Kuwait, there must be at least five directors according to provision 1.1.A of the Kuwait code. The codes in Qatar and the UK do not specify a required number of directors.

Sometimes agreement is reached about a provision, such as the ban against combining the positions of chairman of the board and chief executive officer imposed in Qatari Code Article 7, Kuwaiti provision 1.1.D, Saudi Article 12 provision d, and UK provision A.2.1.[83]

---

[83] Qatar Corporate Governance Code 2009 mentions the traditional relationship between the board and executives by saying that it is assumed that the executives shall prepare plans for the functioning of the company and propose these plans to the board of directors for review, audit and application, which have been approved. Thereafter, the board of directors pursue the application of these plans and ask the executives for performance results.

The country	Main principle	Supporting principle	Articles	Provision
UK	5	18	----- ---	53
Kuwait	11	32	---- ---	More than 235
Qatar	5	-----------	31	Around 85
Saudi Arabia	3	-----------	19	Around 63

Table 5.1 Comparison of the Corporate Governance Codes

Corporate governance code requirements do not distinguish between companies of different sizes. What is appropriate for a large company may not be appropriate for a smaller company, which may find it too costly to comply. One size does not fit all. In the UK, under the 'comply or explain' regime, such a company need not comply. However, where compliance is mandatory, all of the companies are the same.

Under these circumstances, it seems that Kuwait needs two important things. The first is the creation of various bodies, as exist in the UK, to find a proper way to develop and enforce corporate governance principles. The second is deciding the balance between mandatory rules consisting of statutory requirements, such as securities laws and rules, and regulations backed by statute on one hand and principles that operate on a 'comply or explain' basis on the other hand.

8. Enforcement of Corporate Governance

Companies fail because they are poorly managed by the board of directors or because of external risks and factors (the economy, interest rates, exchange rates etc). Accordingly, the law aims to encourage good management by the board. Good corporate governance is a modern subject, and the optimal application of corporate governance helps to reduce these failures. The question here is how to avoid such failures to protect the investors in the long or the short term.

The traditional ways of enforcing corporate governance principles are not suitable for the real world today. The world needs a new framework for the enforcement of corporate governance principles. Through rules and codes, the securities laws can help to form this framework. There is a diversity of enforcement methods. Different aspects of corporate governance are enforced in different ways. Some are enforced by corporate law,[84] while others are dealt with by securities laws[85] and delegated legislation in the forms of rules[86] and voluntary[87] and mandatory codes.[88]

Although a takeover bid is part of securities regulations in Kuwait, and it is an important principle related to corporate governance, it is beyond the scope of this study. This section will look at an example of mandatory rules related to risk management and at the voluntary corporate

---

[84] Kuwait Companies Law 2013; UK Company Act 2006.

[85] UK FSMA 2000; Kuwaiti Law No. 7 of 2010.

[86] Listing Rules; Disclosure Rules; FCA's principles for business (the principles).

[87] UK Corporate Governance Code 2012.

[88] Kuwait Corporate Governance Code 2013.

governance code. Lawmakers have different ideas about how to enforce corporate governance principles. Some prefer to enforce these principles by law, while others prefer to enforce them via a 'comply or explain' regime.[89]

In Kuwait, according to the Corporate Governance Rules 2013, a company must comply and does not have the option of not complying by explaining why it has not complied. Voluntary compliance has advantages for businesses. The nature of business requires a flexible and easily developed means of enforcement, because one size does not fit all. Although the UK is one of the developed countries in the field of corporate governance, corporate governance principles could be enforced by law. However, the British oppose this idea. This can be clearly seen from

---

[89] Applying corporate governance by law has the potential to cause two problems. The first is that it can harm the growth of the economy. The other problem with applying corporate governance principles by law can occur if the company faces financial and administrative burdens as a result of applying all corporate governance principles and consequently needs to employ more staff, spend more money, or gain more legal knowledge about the way to apply these rules and how to bear the cost. Despite this, some countries in Europe have replaced the 'comply or explain' regime with law, because they believe that the board and managers are part of the problem, not part of the solution.

the FRC opinion that applying the 2012 code by law would have some side effects on economic growth.[90] It would be better if Kuwait, Qatar and Saudi followed the example of the UK in terms of applying all of the principles.

Kuwait, Qatar and Saudi issued securities regulations on corporate governance in 2010, 2012 and 2007 respectively. However, Kuwait, Qatar and Saudi securities regulations do not cover some of the corporate governance aspects, such as risk management, and there is no voluntary code which is different from mandatory rules as in the UK.

Board responsibility extends to risk management in many countries. For example, in 2010, the UK extended the board's responsibility for risk to include the nature and the extent of its strategy by deciding the risk facing the business, in addition to the responsibility for the risk of management and control systems according to the Corporate Governance Code.[91] Risk management is not

---

[90] Financial Reporting Council (n 28) 2.

[91] <http://www.charteredaccountants.ie/en/Members/Technical/Corporate-Governance/Corporate-Governance-Articles/Risk-Management-and-

confined to corporate governance code. It is also part of the mandatory principles of business. However, the later do not apply to all issuers. They only apply to certain firms defined as firms "Authorised" by the FCA to offer certain financial products and services including consumer credit firms, banks, investment managers and brokers, insurer and financial advisers. For example, on 9 September 2013, Morgan Chase Bank NA (JP Morgan) was fined £137,610,000 for serious failings related to its Chief Investment Officer (CIO) as a result of high risk taking and weak management causing a £6.2 billion trading loss in 2012.[92] The FCA believed that poor risk management harmed the integrity of the market, as demonstrated by the statement of the FCA's director of enforcement and financial crime, Tracey McDermott,[93] which described this

---

the-new-UK-Corporate-Governance-Code---Bevan-Lloyd-FCA/> accessed 30 November 2013.

[92] <https://www.fca.org.uk/news/jpmorgan-chase-bank-na-fined> accessed 25 June 2015

[93] She stated:

> When the scale of the problems at JP Morgan became apparent, it sent a shock-wave through the markets. Maintaining the integrity of markets is a key part of our wholesale conduct agenda. We consider JP Morgan's failings to be extremely serious such as to

incident as a lesson for all companies.[94] Therefore, this diversity of enforcement (one size does not fit all) depends on the importance of a principle and its impact.

The Corporate Governance Rules 2013 in Kuwait also increased the responsibility of the board of directors by including sound systems for risk management and internal control. This means that the board of directors has the ability to understand and analyse the nature and level of risks to enable the company to reduce them as much as possible. The company is required to provide a number of principles, including creating a department or unit or an independent office of risk management to identify and measure the risks to the company according to Principle 5/1 of the Kuwaiti Corporate Governance Code 2013. The company must also form a committee concerned with risk management according to Principle 5/2 of the Kuwaiti Corporate Governance Code 2013. Saudi Article 10, part (b) 3 of the Code 2006 provides that one of the main

---

undermine the trust and confidence in UK financial markets.

[94]   <https://www.fca.org.uk/news/jpmorgan-chase-bank-na-fined> accessed 25 June 2015

functions of the board of directors is to control and forecast the risk management and to disclose risks with transparency. Comparing Kuwaiti and Saudi codes reveals that the Kuwaiti Code 2013 provides the way to manage the risk by forming a committee and creating a department dedicated to risk management, while the Saudi code leaves to the board of directors the freedom to fulfil its obligations to risk management. Under the 'comply or explain' system, compliance is voluntary. A company cannot face sanctions for non-compliance, only for not explaining its non-compliance. For example, some contend that the UK Corporate Governance Code lacks teeth. Moreover, the UK code allows the company's board a wide discretion for compliance. This idea will be discussed in more detail in the next chapter.

In Article 1 of its 2006 Code, the Saudi legislature clarifies mandatory application by separating principles into optional and mandatory principles and using the 'comply or explain' regime. During the period between 5 October and 7 November 2013, four companies were fined for breaching Article 9, which is entitled 'Disclosure in the Board of Directors' Report', because their board reports did not include the 'comply or explain' system of corporate governance principles.[95] The Saudi code requires disclosure to the shareholders in the boards' reports, as does UK law, while Qatar Article 30 of the 2009 code requires disclosure once a year, and Kuwait requires disclosure four times a year to the Authority.

The Qatari legislature has also adopted the 'comply or explain' regime. Article 2 of the Qatari Corporate Governance Rules 2009 mentions 'the principle of comply or explain non-compliance', which means that the company should disclose the extent of its compliance with the provisions of corporate governance; otherwise, in the case of non-compliance, the company has to determine the material that did not comply and explain the reasons therefore.

In Kuwait, in accordance with part four of Decision No 25 of 2013, the listed companies must provide the Kuwaiti Authority with a report on a quarterly basis about the implementation of these rules, and, if they fail to comply with the rules, the Authority can hold an offender

---

[95] <http://www.cma.org.sa/ar/News/Pages/default.aspx> accessed 11 October 2013.

accountable according to Law 7 of 2007. After passing the new rules about corporate governance in 2013, some people in Kuwait revealed the occurrence of intensive contact between listed companies at the highest levels to prepare for a meeting to lobby against this decision, because everyone was convinced about the impossibility of practical application.[96] The Kuwaiti 2013 code runs to 70 pages, is very detailed and places a heavy compliance burden on companies.

Part of the enforcement of the corporate governance code can be accomplished through listing rules. For example, the British legislature uses listing rules to apply these principles. Therefore, in the UK, if a company does not mention why it did not comply with the rules of governance in its report, it is in violation of the listing rules.[97] The British use this style because the UK Corporate Governance Code is arranged by the Financial Reporting Council (FRC), although the FRC has no power to enforce corporate governance.[98] As a result, some say that one of

---

[96] <http://alwatan.kuwait.tt/ArticleDetails.aspx?Id=296959> accessed 12 August 2013.

[97] Financial Reporting Council (n 28) 15.

[98] Andrew Chambers (n 16) 455.

the real problems with applying corporate governance is how to close the gap between actual implementation and the formal provisions.[99] Diversity in enforcement, including rules and codes, could help.

The best solution for Kuwait to prevent the corporate failures that have afflicted large companies all over the world in terms of securities regulation is, firstly, by creating a new body. Its task should be to develop a corporate governance code over time, such as the FRC in the UK,[100] because corporate governance needs to develop and be reviewed over time.[101] Secondly, Kuwait can use a mix of mandatory and voluntary enforcement mechanisms.

---

[99] Fianna Joesover and Grant Kirkpatrick (n 31) 11-12.

[100] The Corporate Governance Code in the UK is updated every two years. < http://www.frc.org.uk/Our-Work/Codes-Standards/Corporate-governance.aspx> accessed 31 October 2013

[101] The head of the primary markets on the London Stock Exchange, Alastair Walmsley, emphasised that saying that 'we firmly believe that high standards of corporate governance make an important contribution to companies' long term performance. By regularly reviewing and developing appropriate corporate governance practices whatever the prevailing macro-economic conditions'; Alastair Walmsley, 'Corporate Governance for Main Market and AIM Companies' (2012) White Paper, London Stock Exchange 3.

9. Conclusion

This book has focused specifically on these securities laws and regulations as they affect investors in listed companies. This chapter has not attempted to discuss the various theories, such as the agency theory, because the chapter focuses on the real world, which is not adequately explained by any of the theories. In reality, some actions of managers harm investors and other stakeholders, including local communities.

This book has compared the provisions of corporate governance in the UK and those in Saudi Qatar and Kuwait, where, unlike the UK, there is a mixture of mandatory and voluntary rules. By comparing the UK, Saudi and Qatar codes with the Kuwaiti code, some important differences have been found. While the UK uses a principles-based approach, Kuwait uses mandatory rules. The question here is whether voluntary rules would work properly in Kuwait. That will be discussed in the next chapter to determine which rules are better, voluntary or mandatory.

Although the Kuwaiti code could be made voluntary, much work would still be required to explain non-compliance rules. Consequently, one needs to look at how the number of provisions can be reduced. The UK, for example, has 53 provisions, as compared to Kuwait, which has more than 235 provisions. The size of the code is another problem. Some provisions that are in company law are also needed in the code, because an overseas listed company would not be subject to Kuwaiti company law. Kuwait might need a different code for national and international companies. In addition, the Kuwaiti code should distinguish between large and small companies in some provisions, as is done in the UK. Changing the code will take time. However, the financial culture also needs to be changed.

10. Summary and Recommendations

The following is a summary of the main findings, recommendations.

10.1 Summary

Although the Kuwaiti Capital Market Act 2010 does not mention corporate governance, the regulatory authority has used its power to promulgate rules by adopting a corporate governance code. Therefore, this book narrows the scope to the governance issues handled by capital market authorities, especially the codes.

This study has found that there is no clear definition of corporate governance. The literature refers to different components of corporate governance. For example, corporate governance is dealt with in corporate law and as part of securities laws and regulations. This book focused specifically on these securities laws and regulations, as they affect investors in listed companies. It compared the provisions of corporate governance in the UK and in the three GCC countries, where, unlike the UK, there is a mixture of mandatory and voluntary rules.

Although the term 'corporate governance' is used every day in the financial press, it is a complex term. It relates to various fields, such as law, economics, management, accounting and others, and each field has its own developments. Poor corporate governance is a multifaceted subject that involves risk management, bribery, fraud, and poor board practice, all of which can affect listed companies. Some say that the core of the problem is the separation of ownership and control in managing other people's money, which is an agency theory. The need for effective corporate governance rules is greater than ever before. Good corporate governance has the potential to affect both company success overall and the success of the nation. In recent years, a number of scandals and collapses have not only reduced shareholders' financial investment, but have also affected other stakeholders, such as employees who have lost their jobs and, in many cases, their pension funds. Better enforcement methods of corporate governance compliance can limit future lapses in corporate governance and can boost investor confidence, economic efficiency and growth. It is clear that no country is immune from such scandals and collapses, including Kuwait.

This study has found that applying corporate governance principles by means of the law can cause two problems. First, it can harm the growth of the economy. Second, a company faces financial and administrative burdens as a result of applying all corporate governance principles and, consequently, needs to employ more staff, spend more money, and gain more legal knowledge about the way to apply these rules and how to bear the cost. Corporate governance needs to be developed over time. Corporate governance principles do not remain static, but evolve with time and must continue to develop.

Sometimes there is an overlap between the two types of legislation, namely corporate and securities legislation. When a company is listed in the same country as it is incorporated, the company will be subject to both sets of legislation. However, if a company is listed on a stock exchange in a jurisdiction other than where it is incorporated, the company will be held accountable in the jurisdiction where the stock exchange is located according to statutory instruments that apply to that stock exchange.

In the UK, the Finance Reporting Council (FRC) is responsible for publishing the Corporate Governance Code and for promoting high quality corporate governance. The FRC is an independent regulator. However, in Kuwait, the Regulatory Authority is responsible for publishing the code. The 'comply or explain' approach is a key feature of the UK Code. A company cannot face sanctions for non-compliance, only for not explaining its non-compliance. If the company does not mention why it did not comply with the rules of governance in its report, it is in violation of the listing rules.

The majority of the necessary corporate governance rules already exist in Kuwait, but they are not sufficiently wide ranging and have not always adequately protected investors. The securities law could enhance the enforcement of corporate governance principles that can protect investors. Corporate governance in Kuwait is lacking in two areas. First, coverage of various areas of corporate governance, such as risk management, is inadequate. Second, the methods of enforcement of the corporate governance provisions that do exist need to be improved. In Kuwait, compliance with the corporate governance code is mandatory, and failure to comply is a breach of Securities Law No 7 of 2010. Qatar has adopted a 'comply or explain' approach, but the explanation must be provided to the Qatari Capital Market Authority, not the shareholders, in the form of an annual report. In 2006, the Saudi Corporate Governance Code was introduced based on the 'comply or explain' approach. However, over time, certain of the original provisions have become mandatory.

In Kuwait, the corporate governance code requirements do not distinguish between companies of different sizes. What is appropriate for a large company may not be appropriate for a smaller company, which may find it too costly to comply. However, where compliance is mandatory, all of the companies are the same. The Kuwaiti 2013 Code contains 70 pages, is very detailed, and places a heavy compliance burden on companies.

10.2 Recommendations on corporate governance

This book suggests a number of recommendations related to having a good corporate governance code.

10.2.1 Developing a code

An independent organisation should be established to develop a corporate governance code. For example, in the UK, the Finance Reporting Council (FRC) develops corporate governance rules, which are enforced by the FCA, formerly by the FSA. Kuwait would benefit from having an organisation like the FRC to develop a Kuwaiti code.

10.2.2 New framework for enforcement code

The traditional ways of enforcing corporate governance principles are not suitable for the real world today. The world needs a new framework for the enforcement of corporate governance principles. Through rules and codes, the securities laws can help to form this framework. There is a diversity of enforcement methods. Different aspects of corporate governance are enforced in different ways. Some are enforced by corporate law, while others are dealt with by securities laws and delegated legislation in the forms of rules and voluntary and mandatory codes. This thesis has shown that Kuwait needs to balance the mandatory rules consisting of statutory requirements, such as securities laws and rules, and regulations backed by statute on one hand and the principles that operate on a 'comply or explain' basis on the other hand.

10.2.3 Stewardship Code

In the UK, it was felt necessary to introduce a stewardship code for institutional investors. It would be useful to research the feasibility and desirability of introducing such a code in Kuwait.

11. Final observation

This book has made proposals which will provide better corporate governance by making the authorities aware of a number of shortcomings in the current legislation in Kuwait. Hopefully, too, it has added more knowledge to the body of literature in the securities law field, especially for Kuwaiti scholars.

Bibliography

Alan Palmiter, *Securities Regulation: Examples and Explanations* (6th edn, Aspen Publishers 2014).

Alessio Pacces, *Rethinking Corporate Governance: The Law and Economics of Control Powers* (Routledge 2012).

Alpesh Shah, 'Corporate Governance for Main Market and AIM companies' (2012) White Paper, London Stock Exchange.

Andrew Chambers, *Corporate Governance Handbook* (5th edn, Bloomsbury Professional 2012).

Andrew Keay, 'Comply Or Explain: In Need Of Greater Regulatory Oversight', (2012) SSRN Working paper <http://papers.ssrn.com/sol3/papers.cfm?abstract_id=2144132 > accessed 22 February 2014.

Andrew Keay, *The Enlightened Shareholder Value Principle and Corporate Governance* (Routledge 2013).

Andy Ryde, Murray Cox, *The Corporate governance review* (editor Willem Calkoen, 5th edn, Law Business Research Ltd 2015).

Bob Ticker, *Corporate Governance: Principles, Polices and Practices* (3rd edn, Oxford University Press 2015).

Bob Tricker, *The Economist: Directors, An A-Z Guide* (Profile Books 2009).

Brian Cheffins, 'Corporate governance LLM Cambridge, An introduction part 2 (3CL)' (Cambridge University I Tunes).

Chris Gibson-Smith, 'An Essay on the Report Titled 'Comply Or Explain': 20th Anniversary of the UK Corporate Governance Code' (London Stock Exchange, The Financial Reporting Council Limited 2012).

Chris Hodge, 'Corporate Governance for Main Market and AIM Companies' (2012) White Paper London Stock Exchange.

Christine Mallin, *Corporate Governance* (4th edn, Oxford University Press 2013).

David Seidl, Paul Sanderson, John Robert 'Applying "Comply Or Explain": Conformance with Codes of Corporate Governance in UK and Germany' (2009) University of Cambridge working paper.

Donald Nordberg, *Corporate Governance Principles and Issues* (SAGE 2011).

Erik Vermeulen, 'Beneficial Ownership and Control: A Comparative Study - Disclosure, Information and Enforcement' (2013) OECD Corporate Governance Working Papers 7, 8 <http://www.oecd-ilibrary.org/governance/oecd-corporate-governance-working-papers_22230939> accessed 9 September 2013.

Fianna Joesover and Grant Kirkkpatrick, 'The Revised OECD Principles of Corporate Governance and Their Relevance to Non-OECD Countries' (2005).

Gonzalo Puig and Bader Al-haddab, 'The Protection of the Minority Shareholders in the Gulf Cooperation Council' (2013) 13(1) JCLS (123-149).

Luca Enriques and Dirk Zetzsche, 'The Risky Business of Regulating Risky Management In Listed Companies' (2013) European Company and Financial Law Review 10 (3) 1, 2.

Lynn Stout, *The Shareholder Value Myth: How Putting Shareholders First Harms Investors, Corporations, and the Public* (Berrett Koehler Publishers 2012).

82

Massimo Motta, *Competition Policy: Theory and Practice* (Cambridge University Press 2009).

Michelle Edkins, 'Comply or Explain, An Essay on the Report Titled: Comply Or Explain: 20th Anniversary of the UK Corporate Governance Code' (London Stock Exchange, The Financial Reporting Council Limited 2012).

Simon Caulkin, 'Management theory was hijacked in the 1980s' *The Guardian* (London, 28 June 2013) <http://www.guardian.co.uk/commentisfree/2012/nov/12/management-theory-hijacked > accessed 17 October 2013

<http://www.charteredaccountants.ie/en/Members/Technical/Corporate-Governance/Corporate-Governance-Articles/Risk-Management-and-the-new-UK-Corporate-Governance-Code---Bevan-Lloyd-FCA/> accessed 30 November 2013.

'Britain's corporate failures invited a governance revolution' <http://www.ianfraser.org/britains-scandalous-corporate-failures-invite-a-governance-revolution/> accessed 25 October 2013.

Financial Reporting Council (FRC), 'Development in Corporate Governance 2011: The Impact and Implementation of the UK Corporate Governance and Stewardship Codes' (December 2011).

'The 12 Barclays scandals that cast doubt on Diamond's testimony' < http://www.ianfraser.org/move-on-you-crazy-diamond/> accessed 28 October 2013.

<http://www.fca.org.uk/about> accessed 25 June 2015

<https://www.frc.org.uk/Our-Work/Publications/Corporate-Governance/UK-Corporate-Governance-Code-2014.pdf > accessed 24 June 2015.

<https://www.frc.org.uk/Home.aspx> accessed 24 June 2015.

<https://www.fca.org.uk/news/jpmorgan-chase-bank-na-fined> accessed 25 June 2015

<http://www.ft.com/cms/s/0/1a905c28-0aad-11e5-98d3-00144feabdc0.html#axzz3rH8e9NO7> accessed 12 November 2015

< http://www.grant-thornton.co.uk/Global/Publication_pdf/Corporate_Governance_Review_2012.pdf > p6 accessed 25 June 2015

<http://www.londonstockexchange.com/companies-and-advisors/aim/publications/documents/corpgov.pdf> accessed 7 October 2015.

<http://www.theqca.com/about-us/> accessed 12 November 2015.

<http://www.theqca.com/article_assets/articledir_210/105491/QCAResponseFRC_Improving_Quality_Reporting_Smaller_Listed_AIM_Quoted_Companies_Jul15.pdf> accessed 12 Nov. 15